The Role of the Market in Environmental Protection

Brian Meadows

Revive Publications

Copyright © 2011 by Brian Meadows

All rights reserved. This book, or parts thereof, may not be reproduced in any form without permission.

A catalogue record for this book is available from the British Library

ISBN: 978-1-907962-10-3

Published by Revive Publications

Reading, England

For Beth

Contents

Preface

The subject of this book is the degree to which the market and environmental protection are compatible. Can 'market mechanisms' be used to achieve adequate environmental protection? If not, can 'non-market regulations' be imposed on market mechanisms to achieve environmental protection? Alternatively, is adequate environmental protection incompatible with the existence of the market?

The aim of this book is to make some progress in answering these very important questions.

Introduction

What is the relationship between the market and environmental protection? In *Chapter One* I consider the view that the market has a positive role to play in environmental protection. This view includes several elements – neo-classical economics, environmental economics, the tragedy of the commons, the unsustainability of poverty, and the resources for environmental sustainability argument.

In *Chapter Two* I consider the opposing arguments which contend that the market is responsible for environmental degradation and is incapable of environmental protection.

The role of regulations in environmental protection is then considered in *Chapter Three* and these regulations are compared to market instruments. Finally, in *Chapter Four* I discuss the concept of sustainable development and draw some conclusions.

Chapter 1

The Market has a Positive Role to Play in Environmental Protection

The term 'the market' refers to the economic mechanism through which households are free to purchase individual products from firms. When the purchasing decisions of every household are aggregated market forces are generated, these interact with overall supply through changes in price. To understand 'environmental protection' it is necessary to define an 'environmental problem', which is *an anthropogenic induced change to the physical environment which has impacts that society deems to be unacceptable in the light of its shared norms.* Environmental protection can be seen as the counterbalancing anthropogenic attempt to establish ways of preventing environmental problems from becoming too serious, or from occurring in the first place.

In neo-classical economics environmental problems are seen as externalities of production and consumption. These externalities are not included in the market price and are put onto society as a whole rather than the consumers of the product. Pigou argued that governments should tax the creators of negative externalities, the consequent internalisation of societal costs by the creators would then give some environmental protection (van der Straaten, J and Gordon, M, 1995, p. 144). For example, a tax on effluent discharges into rivers would increase the cost of pollution for a factory and thereby cause pollution and social costs to decline. So, a downstream salmon farm would receive some environmental protection from the internalisation.

If society's optimal pollution level is known, along with the costs of additional abatement, then the tax can be set at a level that is concordant with environmental protection. This approach minimises abatement costs, as those firms with the highest abatement costs do the least abatement. Taxes also give firms strong incentives to both develop new technologies, and to increase abatement due to technological progress.

An alternative market approach is the issue of tradable permits, which allow the government to control the overall pollution level whilst also mini-mising abatement costs. An example of tradable permits is the US 1990 Clean Air Act which has reduced sulphur dioxide emissions; the permit price has fallen substantially since trading began in 1998 (Anand, P, 2003, p. 117).

The environmental economics paradigm seeks to assign values to all environmental resources so that they can be fully considered in the neo-classical framework. Without this consideration overuse is likely as many environmental resources are provided free. Environmental economists attempt to obtain optimal values through the use of contingent valuation (CV) surveys. These surveys set up hypothetical markets in order to gauge individuals willingness to pay to save a threatened good (WTP) or their willingness to accept compensation for its loss (WTA). The statistically representational average WTA/WTP figure can then be used in a cost-benefit analysis (CBA) (Burgess, J, 2003, p. 271). Pearce (1989) is convinced that these valuation methods are essential to achieve environmental protection.

A different argument for the necessity of the market for environmental protection relates to the exploitation of common natural resources. Hardin argues that a deficient definition of property rights leads to the overuse of all common property resources, an outcome known as the tragedy of the commons (van der Straaten, J and Gordon, M, 1995, p. 155). He concludes that environmental protection can only be obtained if these common resources are linked to the market through privatisation. For example, this model suggests that global warming occurs because of the lack of property rights to the atmosphere, which causes states to prioritise domestic economic interests over the social benefits from abatement.

It can also be argued that the market offers the best way of achieving environmental protection in the developing countries. These countries suffer from what Terhal (Blowers, A and Glasbergen, P, 1995, p. 166) describes as the *unsustainability of poverty*, with basic needs fulfilment necessitating environmental degradation. As the market stimulates economic growth it follows that it can achieve environmental protection through reducing the *unsustainability of poverty*. However, it is important to ensure that 'quality' growth is obtained, through ensuring equity and minimising both material and energy intensity. In the developed countries it can be argued that the market has been essential in providing the resources for environmental protection. However, to argue that environmental degradation is justifiable on the basis that human capital may be produced which could theoretically be used to repair some of this damage seems to be illogical.

Chapter 2

The Market is Responsible for Environmental Degradation and Incapable of Environmental Protection

Let us now consider the view that the market is responsible for environmental degradation and incapable of environmental protection. The view that the market is responsible for environmental degradation is encapsulated well by Jacobs (1991) who uses the analogy of the market as an 'invisible elbow' which brings general ruin. The deliberate use of the elbow to cause destruction, along with its inadvertent use as individual market decisions are aggregated, can cause severe environmental degradation as there are no environmental constraints in the market mechanism. The presence of market forces also leads to pressure for a constant increase in production. The market thus causes environmental degradation through both the pressures it exerts for material growth, and the high absolute production level resulting from this growth; it is this high level which has caused sustainable environmental constraints to be exceeded.

A fundamental problem of the market is its concentration on short-term economic criteria based on comparative advantage catalysed competition. This results in geographically uneven growth and thus problems of poverty and affluence. These problems make serious the failure of the market to take into consideration the costs of non-renewable resource depletion, which is an example of the inability of the market to take into consideration the needs of future generations. The market is also inadequate because it favours the private interest over the public, and fails to take account of external-ities. These problems imply that the market is intrinsically incapable of long-term environmental protection.

The attempts to seek solutions to this failure through the WTP/WTA valuation methods in environmental economics have serious flaws as studies have shown that respondents do not act rationally in hypothetical markets. A good example is the Central Flyway CV survey in which the average WTP figure for preventing 2000 bird deaths was $80, whilst the figure for saving 20000 deaths was paradoxically lower at $78 (Burgess, J, 2003, p. 271). It can thus be concluded that CV/CBA does not produce robust optimal values. Furthermore, at a more fundamental level the inability to incorporate unpriced scarce resources means that the role of environmental economics in environmental protection is severely limited.

Furthermore, the tragedy of the commons model is found to be limited in its applicability, and as Bromley (van der Straaten, J and Gordon, M, 1995, p. 155) has emphasised the real issue is open access. For example, the tropical rainforest in Brazil was used in a sustainable manner in the absence of property rights, but was significantly deforested following their establishment. Also, open access can simply be restricted to achieve environmental protection, as in the case of the Second North Sea Conference in 1987.

The market failure to account for externalities needs emphasising. The complex and interrelated nature of the causes of many environmental problems makes a comprehensive breakdown of the impacts of each of the 'creators' exceptionally improbable. Furthermore, many environmental goods do not carry a price, and externalities themselves may have differential spatial and temporal impacts. The example of the degradation of the North Sea is a good example of these three factors.

Another important factor is the uncertainty of the effects that an externality has on an ecosystem. For example, the effects of deforestation on future climate are highly uncertain. Whilst the presence of non-monetary external costs – such as the brain damage cause to children by motor exhaust emissions – are important as adequate compensation by the creator is impossible.

The Exxon Valdez disaster highlights another important factor – even if the creator and victims of an externality are obvious, and the creator accepts responsibility for the social costs, and damages are awarded, the immense power resources of transnational companies can mean that internalisation is resisted. In 1989 the Exxon Valdez oil spill occurred; it created monetary externalities as the fisherman of Cordova have foregone incomes of $100,000 a season, and non-monetary externalities due to the illnesses and cancers that have been attributed to the spill and its clean-up. Exxon has used its power to avoid paying out the $5bn awarded to the fishing communities (Gumbel, A, 2004).

Chapter 3

The Role of Regulations in Environmental Protection

The Exxon Valdez case, which was considered in the previous chapter, highlights the need for regulations to achieve environmental protection. Market processes have led to the creation of both large multinational firms and their decisions to use forever bigger supertankers, which exacerbate the risks of environmental destruction. Regulations could limit tanker size and force companies to have immediate clean-up facilities available. An advocate of the deep ecological paradigm may even assert that environmental protection requires regulations to ban supertankers.

These regulations are an alternative to attempts to achieve environmental protection through the market. They generally involve issuing a standard concerning acceptable levels of pollution or types of production technique; an example is the UK Best Practicable Means policy. Regulations are an effective way of achieving environmental targets, and are a necessity when environmental protection is required for irreversible changes, such as biodiversity loss.

An obvious problem with regulations is a lack of effective enforcement. In the Amazon Rainforest there are numerous illegal deliberately started fires that the authorities are incapable of preventing due to a lack of enforcement resources. Furthermore, regulations are less effective at minimising abatement costs than taxes and tradable permits. However, regulations do avoid the problems of enabling major polluters to pay to avoid reducing pollution, as is possible with tradable permits in the Kyoto Protocol.

Chapter 4

The Concept of Sustainable Development

The lesson to be drawn from the previous chapters is that there is a role for both market instruments and regulations in effective environmental protection. This conclusion is part of the motivation underpinning the sustainable development (SD) paradigm. This paradigm has been developed because of the shortcomings of environmental economics. The SD paradigm seeks to achieve environmental protection through maintaining natural resources. Thus the needs of future generations can be accounted for, whilst the problems of externality internalisation and ecosystem complexity are addressed.

SD policies require that ecosystems are used in a way that ensures environmental protection. This means minimising foreign material discharges from stocks, reducing natural material discharges from flows, and limiting anthropogenic space utilisation. This requires policy changes so that we obtain materials and energy from continuing and renewable flow resources in a sustainable manner. Environmental protection thus requires a governmental environmental policy, as the scale and significance of the problems we face cannot be addressed by the market. This policy dictates the level of anthropogenic disruptions that are tolerable, whilst there is a role for both market instruments and regulations in achieving this target. The SD paradigm thus involves a minor role for the market.

However, there are problems with the SD paradigm. These revolve around sustainability definitions and world views. Strong sustainability can be argued to be prohibitively expensive, whilst weak sustainability negates the paradigm (Beckerman, 1994). More importantly the paradigm can be criticised from a deep ecological world view. The SD paradigm ignores the intrinsic value of nature, assumes that the carrying capacities of ecosystems can be calculated, and refuses to challenge the world view of progressive secular materialism (Wooster, 1993).

It can be concluded that the scale of contemporary anthropogenic interference with the biosphere, combined with the limitations of neo-classical environmental economics, mean that the market is incapable of offering adequate environmental protection by itself. The question of whether there is any role for the market depends on the way that the world is socially constructed.

According to an anthropocentric view of the world, which is combined with the ideal of strong sustainability, the SD paradigm can *in principle* give environmental protection; this is possible through the use of regulations and market instruments to meet ecological targets.

However, on an ecocentric view of the world it is possible that there is no role for the market and that environmental protection requires fundamental changes to the global capitalist economic system.

Bibliography

Anand, P. (2003) 'Economic analysis and environmental responses' in Blowers, A. and Hinchcliffe, S. (eds) *Environmental Responses,* Chichester, John Wiley & Sons/The Open University.

Beckerman, W. (1994) '"Sustainable development": is it a useful concept?', *Environmental Values*, vol. 3, no. 3, Autumn, pp. 191-209.

Blowers, A. and Glasbergen, P. (1995) 'The search for sustainable development' in Glasbergen, P. and Blowers, A. (eds) *Environmental policy in an*

International Context: Perspectives, London, Arnold.

Burgess, J. (2003) 'Environmental values in environmental decision making' in Bingham, N., Blowers, A. and Belsham, C. (eds) *Contested Environments,* Chichester, John Wiley & Sons/The Open University.

Gumbel, A. (2004) 'Betrayed by an oil giant', *The Independent,* 25 March, p. 1.

Jacobs, M. (1991) *The Green Economy: Environment, Sustainable Development and the Politics of the Future,* London, Pluto.

Pearce, D. *et al.* (1989) *Blueprint for a Green Economy,* London, Earthscan.

van der Straaten, J. and Gordon, M. (1995) 'Environmental problems from an economic perspective' in Glasbergen, P. and Blowers, A. (eds) *Environmental Policy in an International Context: Perspectives,* London, Arnold.

Worster, D. (1993) 'The shaky ground of sustainability' in Sachs, W. (ed) *Global Economy,* London, Zed Books.

Other books by the author:

Sustainable Development & GM Food: An analysis of the relationship between the genetic modification of crops and the varieties of sustainable development (2011)

Preserving Biodiversity: The role of economics in international environmental policy-making (2011)

www.ingramcontent.com/pod-product-compliance
Lightning Source LLC
Chambersburg PA
CBHW060703280326
41933CB00012B/2289